BASEBALL
Wit

BASEBALL
Wit

by Bill Adler

Crown Publishers, Inc., New York

Grateful acknowledgement is given to Nancy Hogue whose photographs appear on pages 12, 16, 25, 33, 37, 38, 41, 49, 52, 55, 57, 59, 61, 64, 71, 72, 77, 83, 88, 96, 108, 112, 121, and to Ron Modra whose photographs appear on pages 20, 26, 30–31, 45, 63, 95.

Published by Crown Publishers, Inc., 225 Park Avenue South, New York, New York 10003.

Manufactured in the United States of America
CROWN is a trademark of Crown Publishers, Inc.

Library of Congress Cataloging-in-Publication Data
Adler, Bill.
  Baseball wit.
  1. Baseball—Quotations, maxims, etc.   I. Title.
PN6084.B35A35   1986   818'.5402   85-19495
ISBN 0-517-55831-9

Design by Lenny Henderson

10   9   8   7   6   5   4   3   2   1

First Edition

The Innings

FOREWORD . . . vii

1   LINEUP CARDS . . .   1

2   SACRIFICE BUNTS . . . 17

3   WILD PITCHES . . . 31

4   BALKS . . . 39

5   DISPUTED CALLS . . . 56

6   STOLEN BASES . . . 73

7   BEANBALLS . . . 85

8   GROUND RULE DOUBLES . . . 97

9   HOME RUNS . . . 113

Foreword

As the great American game, baseball provides us with a rich depository of truly American humor: wise, salty, ironic, irreverent, and, above all, very funny comments on the game and its special place in the consciousness of the country. *Baseball Wit* records the words of hundreds of players, managers, coaches, owners, umpires, and sportswriters as they praise and defame one another, tout themselves and put themselves down, and, in short, define in a humorous way what it means to love baseball and to compete for its rewards. Whether the game yields heady triumph or abject defeat, it seems that the outrageous barb or the bittersweet riposte is always an essential ingredient. American wit fits baseball like a glove.

1 Lineup Cards

For all its rivalries and passions, baseball is a fraternal game. In **Lineup Cards,** the men of baseball pay colorful tribute both to their teammates and to their respected opponents. Some even pay tribute to themselves.

"I can't very well tell my batters, 'Don't hit it to him.' Wherever they hit it, he's there anyway."

Mets manager Gil Hodges on Willie Mays's prowess in the outfield

⚾   ⚾   ⚾

"He'd hit 'em so high that everyone on the field thought he had a chance to get it. They'd all try to get under it to make the catch, and it looked like a union meeting."

Casey Stengel describes the response to a Babe Ruth pop fly

⚾   ⚾   ⚾

"Yeah, you can pitch him low, but as soon as you throw the ball, run and hide behind second base."

Lou Boudreau, Cleveland Indians manager, gives fatalistic advice on pitching to Ted Williams

⚾   ⚾   ⚾

"Trying to hit Phil Niekro is like trying to eat Jell-O with chopsticks."

Bobby Murcer

⚾   ⚾   ⚾

"I'm not sure I know what the hell charisma is, but I get the feeling it's Willie Mays."

Ted Kluszewski, Cincinnati Reds first baseman

⊗   ⊗   ⊗

"Every time I look at my pocketbook, I see Jackie Robinson."

Willie Mays pays tribute to the breaking of baseball's color bar by Jackie Robinson

⊗   ⊗   ⊗

"Anything that goes that far ought to have a stewardess on it."

Paul Splittorf, pitcher, categorizes a 420-foot George Brett home run

⊗   ⊗   ⊗

"People keep looking for words to describe him. Well, there aren't enough good words or words good enough."

Phil Niekro, then pitching for the Atlanta Braves, on teammate Dale Murphy, 1982 National League MVP

⊗   ⊗   ⊗

"The difference between this guy and the rest of us is that when we get hot, we go up to .300. When he gets hot, he goes up to .500."

Doug De Cinces, Angels teammate, on Rod Carew

⊗   ⊗   ⊗

"It would be presumptuous of me to describe what an artist does. It would be like asking an art student how Michelangelo paints."

Gene Mauch, who managed Rod Carew on both the Twins and the Angels, refuses to try to categorize his talent

Ⓧ   Ⓧ   Ⓧ

"If I was sitting out in the bleachers, I think I'd go get something to eat when he was up. I wouldn't want to get killed."

Steve Kemp on fellow Yankee Dave Winfield's post-All-Star hitting streak, 1983

Ⓧ   Ⓧ   Ⓧ

"He's the only player in baseball who consistently hits my grease. He sees the ball so well, I guess he can pick out the dry side."

Gaylord Perry, on the problems of pitching to Rod Carew ... even with illegal help

Ⓧ   Ⓧ   Ⓧ

"Hitters always have that fear that one pitch might get away from him and they'll wind up DOA with a tag on their toe."

Rudy May, fellow pitcher, pays tribute to Goose Gossage's fastball

Ⓧ   Ⓧ   Ⓧ

"He's the only guy who puts fear into me. Not because he can get me out but because he could kill me."

Reggie Jackson worries about
Nolan Ryan's fastball

⚾   ⚾   ⚾

"One time he hit a line drive right past my ear. I turned around and saw the ball hit his ass sliding into second base."

Satchel Paige on the speed of
Cool Papa Bell when they played
in the Negro Leagues

⚾   ⚾   ⚾

"I got a big charge out of *seeing* Ted Williams hit. Once in a while they let me try to field some of them, which sort of dimmed my enthusiasm."

Rocky Bridges, former infielder

⚾   ⚾   ⚾

"Mathewson pitched against Cincinnati yesterday. Another way of putting it is that Cincinnati lost a game of baseball. The first statement means the same as the second."

Damon Runyon on pitching leg-
end Christy Mathewson

⚾   ⚾   ⚾

"If he was throwing the ball any better, we'd have to start a new league for him."

John Kibler, umpire, on awesome
strikeout pitcher Dwight Gooden
during his 1984 rookie season with
the Mets

⚾   ⚾   ⚾

"There have been only two geniuses in the world. Willie Mays and Willie Shakespeare."

Tallulah Bankhead, actress and baseball fan

① ① ①

"For the first sixty feet it was a hell of a pitch."

Warren Spahn describes the pitch that Willie Mays turned into his first Major League home run, 1951

① ① ①

"It was an insurance run, so I hit it to the Prudential building."

Reggie Jackson modestly describes a home run he hit at Boston's Fenway Park

① ① ①

"He could throw a lamb chop past a wolf."

Bugs Baer remembers pitcher Lefty Grove

① ① ①

"Gibson pitches as though he's double-parked."

Vin Scully, broadcaster, comments on the speed with which Bob Gibson of the Cardinals worked on the mound

① ① ①

"He has muscles in his hair."

Lefty Gomez comments in the 1930s on the strength of Red Sox star hitter Jimmie Foxx

① ① ①

"Some night Zahn's going to deliver the ball, and by the time it gets there, he's going to find out the batter has been waived out of the league or traded."

Bob Lemon, manager, on the slow speed of Geoff Zahn's pitches

Ⓜ   Ⓜ   Ⓜ

"He's like a little kid in a train station. You turn your back on him and he's gone."

Doc Medich, pitcher, on the base-stealing of Oakland's Ricky Henderson, now a Yankee

Ⓜ   Ⓜ   Ⓜ

"Blind people come to the park just to listen to him pitch."

Reggie Jackson gives tribute to Tom Seaver

Ⓜ   Ⓜ   Ⓜ

"That's like asking if I'd rather be hung or go to the electric chair."

Merv Rettenmund replies to a reporter asking whether he'd rather face Tom Seaver or Jim Palmer

Ⓜ   Ⓜ   Ⓜ

"To try to capture Ruth with cold statistics would be like trying to keep up with him on a night out."

Bob Broeg in *The Sporting News*, on Babe Ruth's reputation

Ⓜ   Ⓜ   Ⓜ

"When Steve and I die, we are going to be buried in the same cemetery, sixty feet, six inches apart."

Tim McCarver, Philadelphia Phillies catcher, describes the rapport between himself and pitcher Steve Carlton

Ⓧ   Ⓧ   Ⓧ

"Trying to sneak a fastball past him is like trying to sneak the sunrise past a rooster."

Curt Simmons, Phillies pitcher, on Hank Aaron

Ⓧ   Ⓧ   Ⓧ

"The only way to pitch him is inside, so you force him to pull the ball. That way the line drive won't hit you."

Rudy May, then a Yankees pitcher, on George Brett

Ⓧ   Ⓧ   Ⓧ

"George Brett could get good wood on an aspirin."

Jim Frey, Brett's manager on the Kansas City Royals

Ⓧ   Ⓧ   Ⓧ

"Go up and hit what you see. And if you don't see anything, come on back."

Bucky Harris, Washington Senators manager, on coping with Bob Feller's pitching

Ⓧ   Ⓧ   Ⓧ

"I can see how he won twenty-five games. What I don't understand is how he lost five."

Yogi Berra admits to being impressed with Sandy Koufax after the Dodgers beat the Yankees four games to none in the 1963 World Series

⊗　　⊗　　⊗

"He's baseball's exorcist—scares the devil out of you."

Dick Sharon, Tigers outfielder, on Nolan Ryan's fastball

⊗　　⊗　　⊗

"That's easy. You just take a gun and shoot him."

Ring Lardner, humorist, comes up with a way to stop Ty Cobb from hitting

⊗　　⊗　　⊗

"It was your basic George Foster home run. It probably would have killed four people and broken three seats."

Ed Ott, catcher for the Pirates, after Foster lofted one over the roof

⊗　　⊗　　⊗

"If you saw that pitching too often, there would be a lot of guys doing different jobs."

Joe Rudi, outfielder, on the pitching of Ron Guidry

⊗　　⊗　　⊗

"He threw me his arms, his elbows, his foot, and his wrist, everything but the ball. The next thing I knew, he threw the ball."

Eddie Yost, Washington Senators infielder, on his problems with Satchel Paige's deceptive motion

Ⓧ   Ⓧ   Ⓧ

"The guy's got a fault? Dandruff, maybe."

Leo Durocher has trouble finding a flaw in New York Giants star Frank Malzone

Ⓧ   Ⓧ   Ⓧ

"He isn't much to look at, and he looks like he's doing everything wrong, but he can hit. He got a couple of hits off us on wild pitches."

Mel Ott, New York Giants manager, warns against underestimating Yogi Berra

Ⓧ   Ⓧ   Ⓧ

"[Eddie] Stanky couldn't hit, couldn't run, couldn't field, and couldn't throw, but he was still the best player on the club. All Mr. Stanky could do for you was win."

Branch Rickey, Brooklyn Dodgers executive, knew what was really important

Ⓧ   Ⓧ   Ⓧ

"Jimmie Foxx wasn't scouted, he was trapped."

Lefty Gomez on the discovery of the Hall of Fame slugger

Ⓧ   Ⓧ   Ⓧ

"I've never heard a bat louder than his. You hear it going through the strike zone and the sound is unmistakable. It goes *vump*. That's when he misses."

Ken Harrelson, Red Sox broadcaster, on the swing of Jim Rice

Ⓜ　　Ⓜ　　Ⓜ

"One of these days Howard will unleash a line drive at the opposing pitcher and the only identification left on the mound is going to be a laundry mark."

Fresco Thompson, author of *Every Diamond Doesn't Sparkle*, takes note of Frank Howard's power

Ⓜ　　Ⓜ　　Ⓜ

"Does Pete hustle? Before the All-Star Game he came into the clubhouse and took off his shoes—and they ran another mile without him."

Hank Aaron on Pete Rose's aggressive play

Ⓜ　　Ⓜ　　Ⓜ

"Brooks never asked anyone to name a candy bar after him. In Baltimore, people name their children after him."

Gordon Beard, sportswriter, pays tribute to the great third baseman Brooks Robinson

Ⓜ　　Ⓜ　　Ⓜ

"We tell him, 'Hey, slow down. After you touch home plate there is no other base to run to.' "

Rick Monday on Dodgers teammate Steve Sax

Ⓜ　　Ⓜ　　Ⓜ

"He can brainwash me from sixty feet away."

Tug McGraw on his difficulties in pitching to Pete Rose

Ⓧ　　Ⓧ　　Ⓧ

"Gehrig had one advantage over me. He was a better ballplayer."

Gil Hodges modestly refuses to be compared to the great Lou Gehrig

Ⓧ　　Ⓧ　　Ⓧ

"Without Ernie Banks, the Cubs would finish in Albuquerque."

Jimmy Dykes, Reds manager, paying tribute to "Mr. Cub" in 1958

Ⓧ　　Ⓧ　　Ⓧ

"If we'd known he wanted a car so bad, we'd have given it to him."

Johnny Bench, after Graig Nettles won the MVP award for the American League playoffs

Ⓧ　　Ⓧ　　Ⓧ

"I feel my ability as a ballplayer is overshadowed by people saying, 'Hey, look at that idiot at the plate.' "

Mike Hargrove, nicknamed "The Human Rain Delay" for his maneuvers around the batting box

Ⓧ　　Ⓧ　　Ⓧ

"I guess you could say I'm the redemption of the fat man."

Mickey Lolich, overweight Tiger pitching great

Ⓧ　　Ⓧ　　Ⓧ

"Everybody who roomed with Mickey said he took five years off their careers."

Whitey Ford on Mickey Mantle's reputation for carousing, equaled only by his own

Ⓜ　　Ⓜ　　Ⓜ

"The guy ain't human. Every time he comes to the plate, I keep looking behind to see where it is you wind it up."

Duke Sims, Cleveland catcher, on huge Orioles outfielder Frank Howard, in 1969

Ⓜ　　Ⓜ　　Ⓜ

"Bugs drank a lot, you know, and sometimes it seemed like the more he drank the better he pitched. They used to say he didn't spit on the ball, he blew his breath on it, and the ball would come up drunk."

Rube Marquand analyzes the success of former Giants teammate Bugs Raymond

Ⓜ　　Ⓜ　　Ⓜ

"He gives more signals and signs than the Coast Guard."

Don Riley, sportswriter, comments on the managing style of Gene Mauch of the Angels in 1982

Ⓜ　　Ⓜ　　Ⓜ

"Singe him a little, and the Argentine army could feed off him for a year."

Bud Harrelson, shortstop, on six-foot-eight-inch outfielder Frank Howard

Ⓜ　　Ⓜ　　Ⓜ

"Aw, he's just a regular guy. Except when he eats. Then he's a superstar."

Bruce Benedict, Atlanta Braves catcher, on MVP teammate Dale Murphy

⊗　　⊗　　⊗

"Two-thirds of the earth is covered by water. The other one-third is covered by Gary Maddox."

Ralph Kiner, Mets broadcaster, admires Pirate Gary Maddox's outfield play in 1973

⊗　　⊗　　⊗

"The nice thing about Cesar Cedeno is that he can play all three outfield positions—at the same time."

Gene Mauch, manager, appreciates the mobility of another outfielder

⊗　　⊗　　⊗

"Pete Rose has a twelve-year-old heart inside of a thirty-eight-year-old body."

Tug McGraw, another child at heart

⊗　　⊗　　⊗

"They ought to pay me just to walk around here."

Dave Parker proclaims himself the "foundation" of the Pirates

⊗　　⊗　　⊗

"I'm the straw that stirs the drink."

Reggie Jackson has a clear view of his importance to the Yankees

⊗   ⊗   ⊗

"He's got a gun concealed about his person. They can't tell me he throws them balls with his arm."

Ring Lardner, author and baseball nut, tries to get a fix on Walter Johnson's fastball

⊗   ⊗   ⊗

"My best pitch is anything the batter grounds, lines, or pops in the direction of Rizzuto."

The Yankees' Vic Raschi on the acrobatics of his teammate Phil "the Scooter" Rizzuto at shortstop

⊗   ⊗   ⊗

"Look at Gossage. He's six foot four and most of it is fat. He pitches maybe an inning a week. And for that they pay him a million dollars a year. And you know what? He's worth it."

Rudy May, erratic Yankees starter and long reliever, feels no jealousy about teammate Goose Gossage's fat paycheck

⊗   ⊗   ⊗

"I wish I was half the ballplayer he is."

Al Kaline, future Hall-of-Famer, pays his respects to another, Mickey Mantle

⊗   ⊗   ⊗

2 Sacrifice Bunts

No player, manager, or owner likes to admit a problem, but as we see in **Sacrifice Bunts,** many are capable of admitting their failures and being funny at their own expense.

"They've shown me ways to lose I never knew existed."
                    **Casey Stengel on his expansion
                    Mets**

Ⓧ   Ⓧ   Ⓧ

"My first year and a half there, they were serving a lot of Alpo in the clubhouse."
                    **Tony La Russa on managing the
                    Chicago White Sox**

Ⓧ   Ⓧ   Ⓧ

"Baseball has been very good to me since I quit trying to play it."
                    Whitey Herzog, Cardinals manager

Ⓧ   Ⓧ   Ⓧ

"This losing streak is bad for the fans, no doubt, but look at it this way. We're making a lot of people happy in other cities."
                    **Ted Turner, Atlanta Braves owner,
                    looks for the silver lining**

Ⓧ   Ⓧ   Ⓧ

"I guess I'd better send my fingers to Cooperstown."

**Dennis Lamp, Chicago Cubs
pitcher, after giving up Lou
Brock's 3,000th hit in 1979**

Ⓧ　　Ⓧ　　Ⓧ

"The Good Lord was good to me. He gave me a strong body, a good right arm, and a weak mind."

**Dizzy Dean, at his induction into
the Hall of Fame**

Ⓧ　　Ⓧ　　Ⓧ

"I mighta been able to make it as a pitcher, except for one thing. I had a rather awkward motion and every time I brought my left arm forward I hit myself in the ear."

Casey Stengel

Ⓧ　　Ⓧ　　Ⓧ

"You can't get rich sitting on the bench—but I'm giving it a try."

Phil Linz, utility man

Ⓧ　　Ⓧ　　Ⓧ

"I'm in the twilight of a mediocre career."

**Frank Sullivan, Minnesota Twins
pitcher, in 1962**

Ⓧ　　Ⓧ　　Ⓧ

"You start chasing a ball and your brain immediately commands your body to 'Run forward! Bend! Scoop up the ball! Peg it to the infield!' Then your body says, 'Who, me?' "

**Joe DiMaggio, on how you know
when it's time to retire**

Ⓧ　　Ⓧ　　Ⓧ

"You know, I signed with the Milwaukee Braves for three thousand dollars. That bothered my dad at the time, because he didn't have that kind of dough to pay out. But eventually he scraped it up."

Bob Uecker

Ⓧ   Ⓧ   Ⓧ

"Tomorrow's a new day. If we work hard, we can get back to mediocrity."

Toby Harrah, infielder for the Indians

Ⓧ   Ⓧ   Ⓧ

"I ain't what I used to be, but who the hell is?"

Dizzy Dean, at the end of his career

Ⓧ   Ⓧ   Ⓧ

"We are in such a slump that even the ones that are drinkin' aren't hittin'."

Casey Stengel

Ⓧ   Ⓧ   Ⓧ

"Our backs are to the wall. The Berlin Wall. East Side. But they say Berlin is nice this time of year. Maybe it's time for a great escape."

Dan Quisenberry, reliever, after the Kansas City Royals went two down against Detroit in the 1984 playoffs

Ⓧ   Ⓧ   Ⓧ

"I had some friends here from North Carolina, and they'd never seen a home run, so I gave them a couple."

Catfish Hunter, after he gave up two home runs, pitching against the Dodgers in the 1974 World Series

"You just listen to the ball and bat come together. They make an awful noise."

Darrell Johnson, manager, on when to change pitchers

⚾   ⚾   ⚾

"When you have hands as bad as mine, one hand is better than two."

Ken Harrelson on his rationale for making one-handed catches

⚾   ⚾   ⚾

"It took me seventeen years to get three thousand hits. I did it in one afternoon on the golf course."

Hank Aaron on his golf ability

⚾   ⚾   ⚾

"I was a bonus baby. I got two autographed baseballs and a scorecard from the 1935 All-Star game."

Bob Feller puts modern salaries in historical perspective

⚾   ⚾   ⚾

"The highlight of my career? Oh, I'd say that was in 1967 in St. Louis. I walked with the bases loaded to drive in the winning run in an intrasquad game in spring training."

Bob Uecker

⚾   ⚾   ⚾

"A guy who strikes out as much as I do had better lead in something."

Mike Schmidt, after winning his third consecutive home-run title in 1976

⚾   ⚾   ⚾

"God is still my amigo, but he must be someplace else. Maybe he's watching the American League."

Joaquin Andujar, star Cardinals pitcher, leading both leagues with thirteen losses in July 1983

⊗   ⊗   ⊗

"Why doesn't anyone give me credit? I'm the guy he pinch-hit for both times."

Mike Sadek, reserve catcher on the San Francisco Giants, envies Mike Ivie's two 1978 pinch-hit grand slams

⊗   ⊗   ⊗

"I'm working on a new pitch. It's called a strike."

Jim Kern, reliever

⊗   ⊗   ⊗

"I had my bad days on the field, but I didn't take them home with me. I left them in a bar along the way."

Bob Lemon on how he dealt with the pressures of pitching

⊗   ⊗   ⊗

"Ninety percent I'll spend on good times, women, and Irish whiskey. The other ten percent I'll probably waste."

Tug McGraw budgets a 1975 raise in salary from the Phillies

⊗   ⊗   ⊗

"Our pain isn't as bad as you might think. Dead bodies don't suffer."

Bill Lee sums up the collapse of the Red Sox at the end of the 1978 season

⊗   ⊗   ⊗

"What we're trying to do here is make chicken salad out of chicken shit."

Joe Kukel, Washington Senators manager, during a bad season in 1949

⚾   ⚾   ⚾

"You clowns can go on 'What's My Line' in full uniforms and stump the panel."

Billy Meyer, manager, addresses the woebegone Pirates of the early 1950s

⚾   ⚾   ⚾

"I've had pretty good success with Stan—by throwing him my best pitch and backing up third."

Carl Erskine, Brooklyn Dodgers pitcher, acknowledges his problems getting Stan Musial out

⚾   ⚾   ⚾

"I'm getting by on three pitches now—a curve, a change-up, and whatever you want to call that thing that used to be called my fastball."

Frank Tanana admits he's lost a little speed

⚾   ⚾   ⚾

"If I knew I was going to live this long, I'd have taken better care of myself."

Mickey Mantle celebrates being forty-six

⚾   ⚾   ⚾

"I was a pudgy kid. That was the only place for me to play."

John Gibbons, Mets catcher, on how he got to play that position

⚾ ⚾ ⚾

"Once I tried to drown myself with a shower nozzle after I gave up a homer in the ninth. I found out you can't."

Dan Quisenberry, ace reliever of the Royals

⚾ ⚾ ⚾

"In the long history of organized baseball, I stand un-paralleled for putting Christianity into practice."

Robin Roberts, pitcher, who in 1956 gave up a record forty-six home runs

⚾ ⚾ ⚾

"The fans come to see me strike out, hit a home run, or run into a fence. I try to accommodate them at least one way every game."

Gorman Thomas, outfielder, has a clear grasp of his strengths and weaknesses

⚾ ⚾ ⚾

"Trying to think with me is a mismatch. Hell, most of the time *I* don't know where the pitch is going."

Sam McDowell, Indians pitcher, advises hitters not to try to out-guess him

⚾ ⚾ ⚾

"Sometimes I hit him like I used to hit Koufax, and that's like drinking coffee with a fork."

Willie Stargell, Pirates slugger, admits to problems with pitcher Steve Carlton

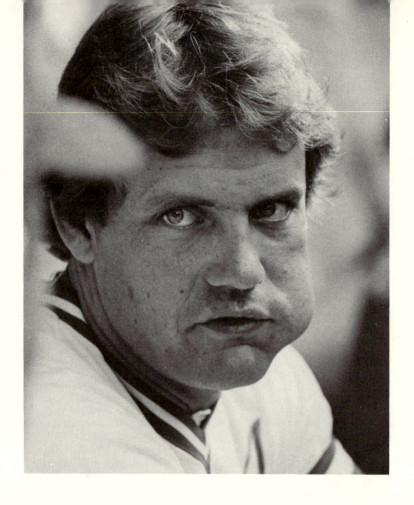

"If I stay healthy, I have a chance to collect three thousand hits and one thousand errors."

**George Brett, during a bad season
at third base**

"I'm just a garbage man. I come into a game and clean up other people's mess."

**Dan Quisenberry is modest about
his job**

"My problem's, uh, behind me now."

George Brett, after surgery for the hemorrhoids that plagued him during the 1980 World Series

⚾   ⚾   ⚾

"Things were so bad in Chicago last summer that by the fifth inning we were selling hot dogs to go."

Ken Brett recalls his 1976 season with the White Sox

⚾   ⚾   ⚾

"That's too bad. They're the only team I can beat."

Dave Cole, pitcher, upon learning that he's been traded to the Phillies in 1955

⚾   ⚾   ⚾

"The fans like to see home runs, and we have assembled a pitching staff for their enjoyment."

Clark Griffith, former Twins executive

⚾   ⚾   ⚾

"Don't ask me how the base-runners got there. I was asleep in the dugout."

Rod Kanehl, pinch-hitting for the 1962 Mets

⚾   ⚾   ⚾

"The only thing we led baseball in was team meetings."

Richie Zisk recalls the 1981 season of the Mariners

⚾   ⚾   ⚾

"We didn't want to weaken the rest of the league."

Frank Lane, general manager of the Brewers, has a reason for not making any trades

①　　①　　①

"I'd rather be lucky than good."

Red Barrett, pitcher, who won twenty-three games for the Cardinals in 1945. The next year he only won three, but the Cardinals won the World Series

①　　①　　①

"The sun don't shine on the same dog's ass all the time."

Catfish Hunter, after he lost a game for the Yankees to the Dodgers in the 1977 World Series. The Yankees prevailed 4–2 for the Series

①　　①　　①

"I was playing it like Willie Wilson, but I forgot that I'm in Clint Hurdle's body."

Clint Hurdle of the Royals knows why he missed a fly ball in the outfield

①　　①　　①

"When you're going like this, it looks like even the umpires have gloves."

Pete Rose, during a hitting slump

①　　①　　①

"Not many people talk to you when you're hitting .195."

**Dwight Evans, during a slump
with the Red Sox, on why he
hadn't gotten a lot of advice from
other players**

⊗　　⊗　　⊗

"The greatest catch I never made."

**Chuck Hiller, Giants infielder,
after outfielder Willie Mays vir-
tually took a fly ball out of his
glove**

⊗　　⊗　　⊗

"You know, it used to take forty-three Marv Throneberry
cards to get one Carl Furillo."

**Marv Throneberry, symbol of the
inept expansion Mets, reflects on
his onetime fan appeal**

⊗　　⊗　　⊗

"First triple I ever had."

**Lefty Gomez is pleased with his
heart bypass surgery, 1979**

⊗　　⊗　　⊗

"I've got a face made for radio."

**Ron Luciano, former umpire, has
an explanation for his lack of success as a color commentator for
NBC television**

⊗　　⊗　　⊗

"This is the biggest thing that ever happened to me. When I'm old and have grandchildren, I can say I was on the other end of the 715th home run."

Tom House, reliever for the Braves, is awestruck after catching teammate Hank Aaron's record-breaking home run in the bullpen

Ⓑ　　Ⓑ　　Ⓑ

"I'm an eclipse player. You don't see me very often."

Benny Ayala, a utility infielder for the Baltimore Orioles, who had been at bat only four times the previous month

Ⓑ　　Ⓑ　　Ⓑ

3 *Wild Pitches*

*J*ust as a pitched ball can get totally out of control, so some of the verbal sallies of baseball people can go completely off course.

"They shouldn't throw at me. I'm the father of five or six kids."

Tito Fuentes, infielder, objects to knockdown pitchers

"I've got a great repertoire with my players."

Danny Ozark, while managing the Phillies

⊗ ⊗ ⊗

"I don't know. I'm not in shape yet."

Yogi Berra, in his playing days, when asked about his cap size at spring training

⊗ ⊗ ⊗

"Baseball and malaria keep coming back."

Gene Mauch, Angels manager

⊗ ⊗ ⊗

"All right, everyone, line up alphabetically according to your height."

Casey Stengel

⊗ ⊗ ⊗

"I'll have to go with the immoral Babe Ruth."

Johnny Logan, shortstop, upon being asked to name the greatest player ever

⊗ ⊗ ⊗

"Every ballpark used to be unique. Now it's like women's breasts—if you've seen one, you've seen 'em both."

Jim Kaat, left-handed pitcher

⊗ ⊗ ⊗

"I want to thank all you people for making this night necessary."

Yogi Berra tries to find the words to express his gratitude during Yogi Berra Night at Yankee Stadium, 1947

⊗ ⊗ ⊗

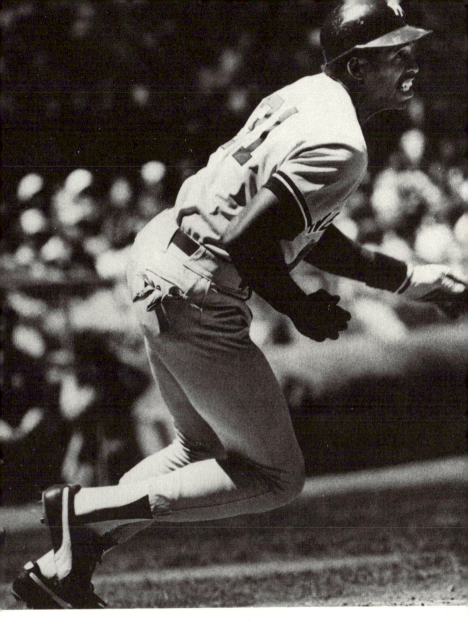

"There's a fly to deep center field. Winfield is going back, back. He hits his head against the wall. It's rolling toward second base!"

Jerry Coleman, Padres broadcaster, loses track of round objects

"There comes a time in every man's life, and I've had plenty of them."

Casey Stengel

⊗　　⊗　　⊗

"I watch a lot of baseball on radio—er, television."

Gerald Ford, former President

⊗　　⊗　　⊗

"He does things that there is no justification for, and then refuses to explain them."

**Tim Foli, Expos infielder, com-
plains about short-lived coach
Karl Kuehl in 1976**

⊗　　⊗　　⊗

"McCovey swings and misses and it's fouled back."

**Jerry Coleman, Padres announcer,
changes the call**

⊗　　⊗　　⊗

"What's the matter with you, Hoyt? You win all your games one to nothing or two to one. Pennock, Bush, Shawkey, those fellows, they win nine or ten to one. Why don't you win some like that?"

**Colonel Jacob Ruppert, Yankees
owner, to pitcher Waite Hoyt in
the late 1920s**

⊗　　⊗　　⊗

"It's so crowded, nobody goes there anymore."

**Yogi Berra explains why he hasn't
been at Toots Shor's restaurant
lately**

⊗　　⊗　　⊗

"The doctors X-rayed my head and found nothing."

Dizzy Dean, after being hit in the head by a baseball during the 1934 World Series

⚾   ⚾   ⚾

"The runners have returned to their respectable bases."

Dizzy Dean, as a radio sportscaster

⚾   ⚾   ⚾

"Rich Folkers is throwing up in the bullpen."

Jerry Coleman, Padres announcer, takes note of warmup activities

⚾   ⚾   ⚾

"Louis Tiant comes from everywhere except between his legs."

Curt Gowdy, sportscaster, comments on the pitcher's distracting windup

⚾   ⚾   ⚾

"Left-handers have more enthusiasm for life. They sleep on the wrong side of the bed, and their head gets more stagnant on that side."

Casey Stengel

⚾   ⚾   ⚾

"There ain't a left-hander in the world that can run a straight line. It's the gravitational pull on the axis of the earth that gets 'em."

Ray Miller, Orioles coach, in 1977

⚾   ⚾   ⚾

"Dissension? We got no dissension. What we ain't got is pitchers."

Roy Campanella, catcher, during a low point for the Brooklyn Dodgers in 1950

Ⓧ   Ⓧ   Ⓧ

"I only go out with girls when I'm horny."

Mark Fidrych, Tigers pitcher, on the clean life, 1976

Ⓧ   Ⓧ   Ⓧ

"How can a pitcher that wild stay in the league?"

Yogi Berra, upon having just struck out swinging on three bad pitches

Ⓧ   Ⓧ   Ⓧ

"Root only for the winner. That way you won't be disappointed."

Tug McGraw knows how to come out feeling happy

Ⓧ   Ⓧ   Ⓧ

"Hot as hell, ain't it, Prez?"

Babe Ruth, upon being introduced to President Harding

Ⓧ   Ⓧ   Ⓧ

"Nice to meet you, King."

Yogi Berra, upon being presented to King George V

Ⓧ   Ⓧ   Ⓧ

"I've never been wrong yet. They just didn't execute what I wanted them to do."

Chuck Tanner promotes the concept of managerial infallibility

⚾   ⚾   ⚾

"How old would you be if you didn't know how old you was?"

Satchel Paige always claimed there was no record of his birth

⚾   ⚾   ⚾

"Congratulations on breaking my record last night. I always thought the record would stand until it was broken."

Yogi Berra leaves out a crucial comma in a telegram to Johnny Bench, after Bench broke Berra's record for the most home runs by a catcher

⚾   ⚾   ⚾

"If this is a ballpark, I'm a Chinese aviator."
**Billy Martin has his say about the
Metrodome**

4   *Balks*

*N*o pitcher likes to make a balk while on the mound; it costs them a base. But off the field, players, managers, and owners alike have been known to complain about everything and anything, making frequent **Balks.**

"If horses don't eat it, I don't want to play on it."

> **Richie Allen, infielder, about artificial turf, 1972**

Ⓑ   Ⓑ   Ⓑ

"In a metropolitan area of about two million, where winter lasts from October to April, being outdoors from May to September is a community event and a mental health imperative."

> **Jay Weiner, sportswriter, offers resistance to the Minneapolis Metrodome in the *New York Times*, 1984**

Ⓑ   Ⓑ   Ⓑ

"The only good thing about playing in Cleveland is you don't have to make road trips there."

> **Richie Scheinblum, former Indians infielder**

Ⓑ   Ⓑ   Ⓑ

"I could never play in New York. The first time I ever came into a game there, I got in the bullpen car and they told me to lock the doors."

> **Mike Flanagan, Orioles pitcher**

Ⓑ   Ⓑ   Ⓑ

"Why should I give the umpires my money?"

Andre Dawson, star Expos out-fielder, explains why he's never been thrown out of a game or incurred a fine

Ⓧ   Ⓧ   Ⓧ

"There goes my wardrobe."

Jason Thompson, Tigers first base-man, reacts to the news that man-ager Sparky Anderson has banned blue jeans

Ⓧ   Ⓧ   Ⓧ

"They got guys playing today with earrings in their ear. If I was still pitching, I'd throw one in their earring."

Billy Loes, former Dodger right-hander

Ⓧ   Ⓧ   Ⓧ

"The only kind of spirit you see today in baseball is the kind you drink."

Johnny Mize, Hall-of-Famer

Ⓧ   Ⓧ   Ⓧ

"When I was a kid, I wanted to play baseball and join the circus. With the Yankees, I've been able to do both."

Graig Nettles

Ⓧ   Ⓧ   Ⓧ

"What's one home run? If you hit one, they are just going to want you to hit two."

Mike Kelleher, Tigers infielder, ex-plains why it's a mistake to even try to hit a home run, which he hadn't

Ⓧ   Ⓧ   Ⓧ

"All last year we tried to teach him English, and the only word he learned was 'million.'"

Tommy Lasorda, Dodgers manager, is unhappy with Fernando Valenzuela's 1982 salary holdout

"Never win twenty games a year, because then they'll expect you to do it every year."

Billy Loes, Brooklyn Dodgers
pitcher, on the importance of
lowered expectations

⚾   ⚾   ⚾

"A manager is like a fellow swimming in the ocean with a cut on his arm. Sooner or later the sharks are going to get him."

Eddie Stanky, after being named
manager of the Rangers in 1977;
he resigned after one day, saying
he was homesick

⚾   ⚾   ⚾

"Most valuable player on the worst team ever? Just how did they mean that?"

Richie Ashburn, who finished his
fine career in the outfield for the
expansion Mets

⚾   ⚾   ⚾

"It's not my life, it's not my wife, so why worry?"

Willie Davis, outfielder, shrugs off
a question about pressure

⚾   ⚾   ⚾

"We used to walk up and down the dugout saying, 'Forget about it, hit the dry side.' He'd throw it twice and you'd be looking for it on 116 pitches."

Earl Weaver suggests that the best
way to deal with Gaylord Perry's
spitter is to ignore it

⚾   ⚾   ⚾

"If you stand next to Perry, he smells like a drugstore."

Billy Martin also has his thoughts about Gaylord Perry

⚾   ⚾   ⚾

"In center field you've got too much time to think about everything but baseball."

Joe Pepitone, who preferred right field

⚾   ⚾   ⚾

"When we played, World Series checks meant something. Now all they do is screw up your taxes."

Don Drysdale, sportscaster and former Dodger pitcher, on how much salaries have risen

⚾   ⚾   ⚾

"The more we lose, the more Steinbrenner will fly in. And the more he flies, the better the chance there will be a plane crash."

Graig Nettles, Yankee third baseman, salutes owner George Steinbrenner's interest in winning during spring training, 1977

⚾   ⚾   ⚾

"Open up a ballplayer's head and you know what you'd find? A lot of little broads and a jazz band."

Mayo Smith in his managing days

⚾   ⚾   ⚾

"I get sick of hearing about the poor owners. Baseball owners today are happier than pigs in slop. They're making money hand over foot."

Earl Weaver

⚾   ⚾   ⚾

"Don't cut my throat. I may want to do that myself."

**Casey Stengel to his barber, when
Stengel was managing the Yankees**

Ⓧ   Ⓧ   Ⓧ

"Superstitious people don't discuss their superstitions."

**Rusty Staub, record-setting Mets
pinch-hitter, refuses to reveal his
secrets**

Ⓧ   Ⓧ   Ⓧ

"They say he hit the gull on purpose. They wouldn't say that if they'd seen the throws he's been making all year. It's the first time he's hit the cutoff man."

**Billy Martin responds to charges
by the Toronto police that Dave
Winfield deliberately threw a ball
at a seagull**

Ⓧ   Ⓧ   Ⓧ

"Baseball is a kids' game that grown-ups only tried to screw up."

Bob Lemon, manager

Ⓧ   Ⓧ   Ⓧ

"Why am I wasting so much time on a mediocre career?"

**Ron Swoboda, outfielder, who
made a spectacular catch in the
1969 World Series, but more often
was plagued with problems**

Ⓧ   Ⓧ   Ⓧ

"We could finish first or in an asylum."

**Frankie Frisch, manager of the
1936 Cardinals "Gas House Gang"**

Ⓧ   Ⓧ   Ⓧ

"There's something about the Yankee uniform that gets you. I think it's the wool. It itches."

> **Joe Gallagher, former Yankee outfielder, puts down the pinstripes**

Ⓧ   Ⓧ   Ⓧ

"People have to learn they can't mess with me."

> **Dwight Gooden, Mets pitcher and 1984 Rookie of the Year, after beating the Cubs 8–1. The Cubs had beaten him in their first game against him**

Ⓧ   Ⓧ   Ⓧ

"If you approach Billy Martin right, he's okay. I avoid him altogether."

Ron Guidry, Yankee pitcher, 1978

"The only thing worse than a Mets game is a Mets doubleheader."

Casey Stengel, in the early 1960s

"Out of what, a thousand?"

Mickey Rivers, after Yankee teammate Reggie Jackson claimed to have an IQ of 160

"They sign for bonuses. If you know where home plate is—$50,000. If you know where first base is—$25,000."

Joe Garagiola, broadcaster, suggests that today's players don't know as much as they should about the game

"With the salary I get here, I'm so hollow and starving I'm liable to explode like a lightbulb if I hit the ground too hard."

Casey Stengel offered this rationale for not sliding in 1918

"Every day in every way, baseball gets fancier and fancier. A few more years and they'll be playing on oriental rugs."

Russell Baker, columnist, disapproves of the direction the game has taken

"The Mets always said I couldn't win the big games. I'd like to know the last time the Mets *had* a big game."

Pete Falcone, former Mets pitcher, after being traded to the Braves

⊗   ⊗   ⊗

"Some of the bugs there are twin-engine jobs."

Sandy Koufax, in pre-Astrodome days, on one of the problems with playing in Houston

⊗   ⊗   ⊗

"I don't want any doctor building a swimming pool with my knee."

Steve Howe of the Dodgers balks at having an operation

⊗   ⊗   ⊗

"You don't always *make* an out. Sometimes the pitcher *gets* you out."

Carl Yastrzemski, the only 400-home-run, 3,000-hit player from the American League, during a slump

⊗   ⊗   ⊗

"It's tough to sit in that on-deck circle making $800,000 less than somebody hitting in front of you."

Reggie Jackson, unhappy about Dave Winfield's huge Yankee contract

⊗   ⊗   ⊗

"This isn't the College World Series. With 27,000 bucks on the line, I hate everybody."

Ken Holtzman, Oakland A's pitcher

⊗   ⊗   ⊗

"I don't walk the streets."

Bruce Kison, Pirates pitcher, gives short shrift to a reporter's question about how often he was recognized on the street

⚾ ⚾ ⚾

"A lot of them come out to scream at players. They can't scream at their wife at home. So they come out here, have a couple of beers, and scream."

Rod Carew attributes the abusive behavior of fans to personal frustrations

⚾ ⚾ ⚾

"The Goose should do more pitching and less quacking."

George Steinbrenner, Yankees owner, complains about Goose Gossage's complaints, 1982

⚾ ⚾ ⚾

"Damn, I'm going so bad that I don't even get thrown out of the game right. Aren't they supposed to give you a chance to stand around and argue?"

Oscar Gamble, hitting miserably for the Yankees in 1981, manages to change the subject to umpiring

⚾ ⚾ ⚾

"I have some good news and some bad news. The good news is that we've outdrawn the Dodgers. The bad news is that I've never seen such stupid ballplaying in my life."

Ray Kroc, after buying the Padres, speaks over the public-address system to the opening-day crowd

⚾ ⚾ ⚾

"I loved the game. I loved the competition. But I never had any fun. I never enjoyed it. All hard work, all the time."

Carl Yastrzemski looks back with gloom during his final season, 1983

49

"I got a million dollars worth of free advice and a very small raise."

Eddie Stanky of the Brooklyn Dodgers is a little dazed after dealing with notoriously tight-fisted Dodger executive Branch Rickey in 1945

"So many guys come and go here that if we won the pennant, our shares would be fifty dollars apiece."

Danny Cater is bemused by the constant roster changes on the 1975 Cardinals

"What do you want me to do? Let them sons of bitches stand up there and think on my time?"

Grover Cleveland Alexander, Hall of Fame pitcher, had his reasons for wasting no time between pitches

"How can I intimidate batters if I look like a goddamn golf pro?"

Al Hrabosky, the reliever known as the Mad Hungarian, objects to an order to get rid of his wild mustache and sideburns

"Now, they talk on the radio about the records set by Ruth and DiMaggio and Henry Aaron. But they rarely mention mine. Do you know what I have to show for the sixty-one home runs? Nothing, exactly nothing."

Roger Maris displays a smidgin of bitterness about the treatment given his home-run record

⚾   ⚾   ⚾

"Neil, don't you know, young man, that I've had a bypass? You have to take it easy on me."

George Bamberger, while manager of the Mets, tries to persuade relief pitcher Neil Allen to stop getting into so many jams on the mound

⚾   ⚾   ⚾

"I will be the first manager in history who will be twenty-five games dumber before the first ball is thrown out."

Whitey Herzog, Cardinals manager, complains that the free-agency clause might lose him Bruce Sutter, who had forty-five saves for the team in 1984

⚾   ⚾   ⚾

"One of the chief duties of the fan is to engage in arguments with the man behind him. This department of the game has been allowed to run down fearfully."

Robert Benchley, writer and member of the famous Algonquin Round Table collection of wits

⚾   ⚾   ⚾

"He didn't sound like a baseball player. He said things like 'Nevertheless,' and 'If, in fact.' "

Dan Quisenberry, pitcher, is amused by the educated lingo of catcher Ted Simmons

Ⓧ   Ⓧ   Ⓧ

"I still think neckties are designed to get in your soup."

Ted Williams continues to ride a favorite hobbyhorse

⚾   ⚾   ⚾

"It's a good thing Babe Ruth isn't still here. If he was, George would have him bat seventh and tell him he's overweight."

Graig Nettles takes on George Steinbrenner once again

⚾   ⚾   ⚾

"Are you trying to insult Hubbell—coming up here with a bat?"

Gabby Hartnett, umpire, twits pitcher Lefty Gomez as he comes up to the plate to bat against his great rival, Carl Hubbell, in 1934

⚾   ⚾   ⚾

"Nowadays they have more trouble packing hair dryers than baseball equipment."

Bob Lemon doesn't like what's happened to the game

⚾   ⚾   ⚾

"If they think I'd stand there in that sun and pitch another nine innings waiting for our bums to make another run, they're crazy."

Jack Nabors of the Athletics had a sound reason for walking in the winning run in 1916. The score was tied 1-1 in the ninth inning.

⚾   ⚾   ⚾

"Ted Kluszewski was on third. Somebody like Odrowski on second, maybe Timowitz on first. Boy, was I sweatin', hopin' nobody'd get a hit and I wouldn't have to call all those names."

Dizzy Dean, who had trouble enough with common names, in his broadcasting days

Ⓧ   Ⓧ   Ⓧ

"I don't need an agent. Why should I give somebody ten percent when I do all the work?"

Mark Fidrych, Detroit pitcher, before injuries knocked him out of the game for good

Ⓧ   Ⓧ   Ⓧ

"I've always felt a lot of pitching coaches made a living out of running pitchers so they wouldn't have to spend that same time teaching them how to pitch."

Johnny Sain, himself a pitching coach, takes issue with exercise for its own sake

Ⓧ   Ⓧ   Ⓧ

"If they worked as hard at their jobs as I do at mine, this country wouldn't have the inflation problem it has now."

Mike Marshall, pitcher, resents fans who boo

Ⓧ   Ⓧ   Ⓧ

"A well-paid slave is nonetheless a slave."

Curt Flood challenges baseball's trading system in 1970

Ⓧ   Ⓧ   Ⓧ

5 *Disputed Calls*

The umpire makes a call. Players and managers disagree vehemently. "Safe!" "Out!" But umpires aren't the only baseball people who sometimes make **Disputed Calls.**

"If the people don't want to come out to the park, nobody's going to stop them."

Yogi Berra

ⓧ   ⓧ   ⓧ

"We are here to prove there is no Santa Claus."

> **Brooks Robinson, Orioles third baseman, before the start of the 1969 World Series against the "Miracle Mets," who took the Series**

ⓧ   ⓧ   ⓧ

"If a guy's a good pitcher, he's going to play good anywhere. We can play in Istanbul."

> **Larry Bowa of the Cubs before the 1984 playoffs against the Padres. The Cubs took the first two games in San Diego, but then blew three at home**

ⓧ   ⓧ   ⓧ

"There's a good crowd tonight. I was going to say people were strung out all over the place, but people might take that literally."

Hank Greenwald, Giants announcer, being cautious with language, 1981

"The way to catch a knuckleball is to wait until the ball stops rolling and then pick it up."

Bob Uecker, comedian and former catcher

"I wouldn't have a problem with him, though. I don't have to get him out."

Bruce Sutter of the Cardinals, after opting for free-agency in 1984, considers the possibility of pitching for George Steinbrenner's Yankees

Ⓧ   Ⓧ   Ⓧ

"I didn't come to New York to be a star. I brought my star with me."

Reggie Jackson, after signing with the Yankees

Ⓧ   Ⓧ   Ⓧ

"I don't really go to compete. I go to be seen."

Reggie Jackson on the importance of the All-Star game

Ⓧ   Ⓧ   Ⓧ

"It's nice, pitching in an airport."

Vida Blue, praising the vast outfield spaces in Oakland

Ⓧ   Ⓧ   Ⓧ

"Fractured, hell! The damn thing's broken."

Dizzy Dean knew what had happened to his toe

Ⓧ   Ⓧ   Ⓧ

"Baseball is ninety percent mental. The other half is physical."

Yogi Berra sums it up

Ⓧ   Ⓧ   Ⓧ

"I lost it in the sun."

**Billy Loes, former Dodgers right-
hander, has an alibi for bobbling a
ground ball**

Ⓜ   Ⓜ   Ⓜ

"I'm like an old tin can in an alley. Anyone who walks by
can't resist kicking it."

**Donald M. Grant, former Mets
owner who traded away Jerry
Koosman, Nolan Ryan, and Tom
"the Franchise" Seaver**

Ⓜ   Ⓜ   Ⓜ

"We made too many wrong mistakes."

**Yogi Berra, on why the Yankees
lost to the Dodgers in the 1960
World Series**

Ⓜ   Ⓜ   Ⓜ

"I'd walk through hell in a gasoline suit to keep playing
baseball."

Pete Rose

Ⓜ   Ⓜ   Ⓜ

"Not intentionally, but I sweat easy."

**Lefty Gomez, when asked if he
threw a spitter**

Ⓜ   Ⓜ   Ⓜ

"Managers really encouraged players to talk it up on the
bench. That was important. You had to keep those guys
from falling asleep, because I've seen guys fall right off
that bench and onto the disabled list."

Bob Feller recalls his playing days

Ⓜ   Ⓜ   Ⓜ

"It has always been my ambition to play in New York City. Brooklyn is all right, but if you're not with the Giants, you might as well be in Albany."

Bill Dahlen, Giants shortstop, in the days of the great rivalry with the Brooklyn Dodgers

Ⓑ   Ⓑ   Ⓑ

"I'd always have it in at least two places, in case the umpires would ask me to wipe one off. I never wanted to be caught out there without anything. It wouldn't be professional."

Gaylord Perry, author of Me and The Spitter

Ⓑ   Ⓑ   Ⓑ

"There's much less drinking now than there was before 1927, because I quit drinking on May 24, 1927."

Rabbit Maranville, infielder for the Boston Braves, 1928

Ⓑ   Ⓑ   Ⓑ

"If I were a Tibetan priest and ate everything perfect, maybe I'd live to be 105. The way I'm going now, I'll probably only make it to 102. I'll give away three years to beer."

Bill Lee, Red Sox and Expos left-hander

Ⓑ   Ⓑ   Ⓑ

"I like a little conflict."

George Steinbrenner, Yankees owner, understates the case in 1978

Ⓑ   Ⓑ   Ⓑ

"You never know with these psychosomatic injuries. You have to take your time with them."

Jim Palmer, Cy Young Award pitcher

⚾   ⚾   ⚾

"Them ain't lies. Them's scoops."

Dizzy Dean responds to the charge that he tells every reporter a different place when asked where he was born

⚾   ⚾   ⚾

"Asking him to be an impartial play-by-play announcer would be no different from sending Captain Ahab after bay scallops."

Vic Zeigel, sportswriter, on Phil "Holy Cow" Rizzuto's partisan style

⚾   ⚾   ⚾

"An hour after the game, you want to go out and play them again."

Rocky Bridges, coach, on playing the Japanese

⚾   ⚾   ⚾

"It takes him an hour and a half to watch '60 Minutes.' "

Donald Davidson, Astros executive, marveling at Joe Niekro's ability to relax

⚾   ⚾   ⚾

"There goes Rick Monday. He and Manny Mota are so old that they were waiters at the Last Supper."

Tommy Lasorda, manager of the Dodgers, on the two "old men" of his team

① ① ①

"The only thing running and exercising can do for you is make you healthy."

Mickey Lolich

① ① ①

"It seems to me the official rule book should be called the funny pages. It obviously doesn't mean anything. The rule book is only good for you when you go deer hunting and run out of toilet paper."

Billy Martin comments on an especially bad week, even for him, with the umpires

① ① ①

"Being with a woman all night never hurt no professional baseball player. It's staying up all night looking for a woman that does him in."

Casey Stengel

① ① ①

"I immediately got the feeling I was wrong on the call when every Baltimore guy on the field charged at me with intent to maim."

Ron Luciano, former umpire, on miscalling a foul ball as a home run

① ① ①

"300 Wins Is Nothing to Spit At."

Gaylord Perry's T-shirt the day he won his 300th game, pitching for the Seattle Mariners

⊗   ⊗   ⊗

"Ruth made a big mistake when he gave up pitching. Working once a week, he might have lasted a long time and become a great star."

Tris Speaker, Cleveland coach, when Babe Ruth switched to the outfield

⊗   ⊗   ⊗

"Anytime I got those bang-bang plays at first base, I called them out. It made the game shorter."

Tommy Gorman, former umpire

⊗   ⊗   ⊗

"I didn't want to win it by sneaking in the back door, but I did sneak in the back door. My pride told me to play, but my common sense told me not to. I went with my common sense."

Willie Wilson of the Royals, discussing his down-to-the-wire race with Robin Yount of the Brewers for the 1982 batting title. Wilson decided to sit out the final game of the season. The result: Wilson took the title .3316 to Yount's .3307.

⊗   ⊗   ⊗

"Who's on first, What's on second, I Don't Know is on third."

Bud Abbott to Lou Costello

⊗   ⊗   ⊗

"Why pitch nine innings when you can get just as famous pitching two?"

Sparky Lyle, ace reliever

① ① ①

"I am dead set against free-agency. It can ruin baseball."

George Steinbrenner, before becoming the biggest dipper in the free-agency market

① ① ①

"Cut me and I'll bleed Dodger blue."

Tommy Lasorda, manager, either showing his loyalty or aspiring to royalty

① ① ①

"I don't know why, but I can run faster in tight pants."

Phil Linz, infielder, forgetting that he spent most of his time on the bench

① ① ①

"There is one word in America that says it all, and that one word is, 'You never know.' "

Joaquin Andujar, pitcher, tries to make a point in English

① ① ①

"I'd rather play in hell than for the Angels."

Alex Johnson, who ultimately had his greatest success as an Angel, winning the 1970 American League batting championship with a .328 average

① ① ①

"People have the most fun when they're busting their ass."

Ted Turner, Atlanta Braves owner, a believer in the work ethic

⊗ ⊗ ⊗

"All pitchers are liars and crybabies."

Yogi Berra thinks too many pitchers disagree with the work ethic

⊗ ⊗ ⊗

"I have given Mike Cuellar more chances than my first wife."

Earl Weaver, during Cuellar's disastrous 1976 season for the Orioles

⊗ ⊗ ⊗

"When I get through managing, I'm going to open up a kindergarten."

Billy Martin considers an unlikely career change

⊗ ⊗ ⊗

"We have deep depth."

Yogi Berra

⊗ ⊗ ⊗

"One long-ball hitter, that's what we need. I'd sell my soul for one long-ball hitter—hey, where did you come from?"

Robert Shafer, fictional manager of the Washington Senators, to Mr. Applegate, otherwise known as the Devil, in the musical *Damn Yankees*

⊗ ⊗ ⊗

"It gets late early out there."

**Yogi Berra, attempting to explain
the shadows in Yankee stadium**

⚾   ⚾   ⚾

"The biggest problem I've had is that I can't figure out a
way to spend my forty-three-dollars-a-day meal money.
No matter what I do, I can't spend it."

**Andy Van Slyke, Cardinal rookie
in 1983, in need of a gourmet restaurant guide**

⚾   ⚾   ⚾

"I won't play for a penny less than fifteen hundred dollars."

**Homus Wagner, Hall-of-Famer, in
need of arithmetic lessons, turning
down a salary offer of $2,000 a
year early in his career**

6 *Stolen Bases*

The pitcher releases the ball, and before he knows it, the runner at first is the runner at second. Baseball people off the field can sometimes get by with verbal **Stolen Bases.**

"You couldn't play on my Amazing Mets without having held some kind of record, like one fella held the world's international all-time record for a pitcher getting hit on the ankles."

Casey Stengel never did get over the shock of managing the Mets

Ⓧ   Ⓧ   Ⓧ

"If I'd done everything I was supposed to, I'd be leading the league in homers, have the highest batting average, have given $100,000 to the Cancer Fund, and be married to Marie Osmond."

Clint Hurdle, outfielder, reviews his rookie year with the Royals, 1978

Ⓧ   Ⓧ   Ⓧ

"I'd get me a bunch of bats and balls and sneak me a couple of umpires and learn them kids behind the Iron Curtain how to tote a bat and play baseball."

Dizzy Dean, in his broadcasting days, comes up with a simple solution to communism

Ⓧ   Ⓧ   Ⓧ

"He should be in the Hall of Fame, with a tube of K-Y Jelly attached to his plaque."

Gene Mauch, manager, pays tribute to pitcher Gaylord Perry, sort of

Ⓧ   Ⓧ   Ⓧ

"The Yankees . . . are a family. A family like the Macbeths, the Borgias, and the Bordens of Fall River, Mass."

Ron Fimrite, writer for *Sports Illustrated*

Ⓧ   Ⓧ   Ⓧ

"He talks very well for a guy who's had two fingers in his mouth all his life."

Gene Mauch, manager, analyzes former pitcher Don Drysdale's ability as a broadcaster in terms of his reputation for throwing spitballs

Ⓧ   Ⓧ   Ⓧ

"I owe my success to expansion pitching, a short right-field fence, and my hollow bats."

Norm Cash, twenty years after winning the American League batting title in 1961, demonstrates how to turn a sacrifice bunt into a stolen base, verbally speaking

Ⓧ   Ⓧ   Ⓧ

"Felt pretty good when I got up this morning. But I got over it."

Smokey Burgess, White Sox catcher, 1967

Ⓧ   Ⓧ   Ⓧ

"I had no trouble communicating. The players just didn't like what I had to say."

Frank Robinson, Hall of Fame outfielder, and the first black manager, on his managerial debut with the Indians

① ① ①

"Errors are a part of my image."

Dick Stuart, Phillies shortstop, finds a reason for his erratic glove

① ① ①

"When I first became a manager, I asked Chuck for advice. He told me, 'Always rent.' "

Tony La Russa, then White Sox manager, reporting on the wise words of longtime manager Chuck Tanner

① ① ①

"The best qualification a coach can have is being the manager's drinking buddy."

Jim Bouton, author of the book *Ball Four*, shows his respect for coaches

① ① ①

"Being traded is like celebrating your hundredth birthday. It might not be the happiest occasion in the world, but consider the alternatives."

Joe Garagiola, broadcaster

① ① ①

"Between owners and players, a manager today has become a wishbone."

John Curtis, pitcher

① ① ①

"Rooting for the New York Yankees is like rooting for U.S. Steel."

Red Smith, sportswriter, during the heyday of the Yankees, 1951

⊗ ⊗ ⊗

"The great thing about baseball is that there's a crisis every day."

Gabe Paul, baseball executive

⊗ ⊗ ⊗

"The only reason I don't like playing in the World Series is I can't watch myself play."

Reggie Jackson, "Mr. October"

⊗ ⊗ ⊗

"He is easily the slowest ballplayer since Ernie Lombardi was thrown out at first base trying to stretch a double into a single."

Stanley Frank, sportswriter, finds a way to describe the speed of Lou Boudreau

⊗ ⊗ ⊗

"What are we doing, getting new lightbulbs for Lemon's nose?"

Graig Nettles, referring delicately to the drinking habits of Yankee manager Bob Lemon, when Lemon asked for the team bus to make an unscheduled stop

⊗ ⊗ ⊗

"You don't save a pitcher for tomorrow. Tomorrow it may rain."

Leo Durocher displays impeccable logic

⊗ ⊗ ⊗

"Dark throws stools; Hutch throws rooms."

**Ed Bailey, Reds catcher, compares
the managerial temperaments of
Alvin Dark and Fred Hutchinson**

Ⓟ   Ⓟ   Ⓟ

"I don't throw the first punch. I throw the second four."

Billy Martin on off-duty pugilism

Ⓟ   Ⓟ   Ⓟ

"Did you ever see a monkey with a cramp?"

**Bill Lee defends his banana diet
while pitching for the Expos in
1979**

Ⓟ   Ⓟ   Ⓟ

"My best pitch is one I do not throw."

Lew Burdette, pitcher, pretending there is no such thing as a spitball

⊗   ⊗   ⊗

"I'm a light eater. When it gets light, I start eating."

Tommy John, pitcher

⊗   ⊗   ⊗

"The boy's got talent and desire, but he ain't got no neck."

John McGraw, Giants manager, is unimpressed with the physical appearance of stocky Hack Wilson

⊗   ⊗   ⊗

"I've seen him order everything on the menu except 'Thank you for dining with us.'"

Jerry Royster comments on Braves teammate Dale Murphy's appetite

⊗   ⊗   ⊗

"I took a little English, a little math, some science, a few hubcaps, and some wheelcovers."

Gates Brown, outfielder, discusses his high school days

⊗   ⊗   ⊗

"Never trust a baseman who's limping. Comes a base hit and you'll think he just got back from Lourdes."

Joe Garagiola, broadcaster

⊗   ⊗   ⊗

"Mike Ivie is a forty-million-dollar airport with a thirty-dollar control tower."

Rick Monday needles a Dodger teammate

⊗   ⊗   ⊗

"I got a kid, Greg Goosen, he's nineteen years old and in ten years he's got a chance to be twenty-nine."

Casey Stengel appraises some new talent on the 1965 Mets

Ⓜ Ⓜ Ⓜ

"Having Marv Throneberry play for your team is like having Willie Sutton play for your bank."

Jimmy Breslin, columnist, finds another way of summing up the dubious talents of the Mets' "Marvelous Marv"

Ⓜ Ⓜ Ⓜ

"He's even-tempered. He comes to the ballpark mad and stays that way."

Joe Garagiola, sportscaster, on hard-hitting shortstop Rick Burleson

Ⓜ Ⓜ Ⓜ

"This wouldn't be such a bad place to play if it wasn't for that wind. I guess that's like saying hell wouldn't be such a bad place if it wasn't so hot."

Jerry Reuss, Dodgers pitcher, on the drawbacks of San Francisco's Candlestick Park

Ⓜ Ⓜ Ⓜ

"I wish I could buy you for what you're really worth, and sell you for what you think you're worth."

Mickey Mantle proves that the country boy isn't so dumb, as he addresses teammate Joe Pepitone

Ⓜ Ⓜ Ⓜ

"I like my players to be married and in debt. That's the way you motivate them."

Ernie Banks, Hall-of-Famer, getting a handle on being a minor-league manager

Ⓧ   Ⓧ   Ⓧ

"If a manager of mine ever said someone was indispensable, I'd fire him."

Charles C. Finley gave undue credit to no man

Ⓧ   Ⓧ   Ⓧ

"I'm not a great runner. I'm no Joe Morgan, but I'm not bad for a white guy."

Pete Rose is no racist

Ⓧ   Ⓧ   Ⓧ

"Statistics are about as interesting as first-base coaches."

Jim Bouton pulls a fast comparison

Ⓧ   Ⓧ   Ⓧ

"I'm going to buy the Suez Canal. When one of his ships comes through there, I'm going to blow it up."

Dock Ellis, while on the Yankee pitching staff, plans to cope with owner George Steinbrenner by taking out one of the foundations of his fortune

Ⓧ   Ⓧ   Ⓧ

"All literary men are Red Sox fans. To be a Yankee fan in literary society is to endanger your life."

John Cheever, distinguished author, giving a new twist to an ancient rivalry

Ⓧ   Ⓧ   Ⓧ

"As I remember it, the bases were loaded."

Garry Maddox, Phillies outfielder, comments expansively on a grand-slam home run

⚾   ⚾   ⚾

"Gaylord is a very honorable man. He only calls for the spitball when he needs it."

Gabe Paul, baseball executive, has Gaylord Perry's number

⚾   ⚾   ⚾

"His trouble is he takes life too seriously. Cobb is going at it too hard."

Cy Young, legendary pitcher, chides legendary hitter Ty Cobb

⚾   ⚾   ⚾

"I always liked working Indian games, because they were usually out of the pennant race by the end of April and there was never too much pressure on the umpires."

Ron Luciano, in *The Umpire Strikes Back*, explains why he liked going to Cleveland

⚾   ⚾   ⚾

"Let me give you a tip, Yogi. The opera's not over until the fat lady sings."

Sal Marciano, NBC sportscaster, to Yogi Berra outside the Metropolitan Opera House. Yogi had just been rehired as Yankee manager for 1985 and was about to attend a performance of *La Bohème* with his wife, Carmen.

⚾   ⚾   ⚾

"If Houston and Montreal stay on top, it will be the first time the National League playoffs take place entirely outside the United States."

Hank Greenwald, sportscaster, steals one standing up during the 1979 pennant race

Ⓧ   Ⓧ   Ⓧ

"You have two hemispheres in your brain—a left and a right side. The left side controls the right side of your body and the right controls the left half. It's a fact. Therefore, left-handed pitchers are the only people in their right minds."

Bill Lee, left-handed pitcher, counters the idea that he is a "flake"

Ⓧ   Ⓧ   Ⓧ

"I'm the most loyal player money can buy."

Don Sutton, pitcher, has a keen grasp of free-agency

Ⓧ   Ⓧ   Ⓧ

"This club is a lot of fun, like my wife, but there's no profit in either one."

Ray Kroc, late owner of the Padres

Ⓧ   Ⓧ   Ⓧ

"I think it's wonderful. It keeps the kids out of the house."

Yogi Berra pays his respects to Little League baseball

Ⓧ   Ⓧ   Ⓧ

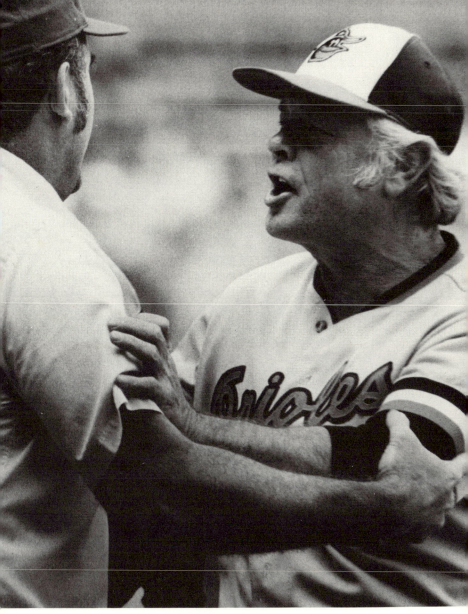

"Bad baseball players make good managers."
Earl Weaver, bad player, great manager

"How can a guy win a game if you don't give him any runs?"

Bo Belinsky finding another way to look at it when he was behind 15–0

ⓧ   ⓧ   ⓧ

"They examined all my organs. Some of them are quite remarkable, and others are not so good. Several museums are bidding on them."

Casey Stengel gets out of a run-down with his doctors

ⓧ   ⓧ   ⓧ

"Look, we play 'The Star-Spangled Banner' before every game. You want us to pay taxes, too?"

Bill Veeck, Cubs owner, doesn't like the tax system any more than baseball under the lights

ⓧ   ⓧ   ⓧ

"Play me or keep me."

Phil Linz, Yankee utility player, lacked the clout to demand a trade

ⓧ   ⓧ   ⓧ

"He is the guts of the Angels, our triple threat. He can hit, run, and lob."

Merv Rettenmund assesses the throwing ability of sore-armed teammate Don Baylor

ⓧ   ⓧ   ⓧ

7 _Beanballs_

he ball is coming right at the batter's head, and suddenly he's in the dust. Sometimes **Beanballs** get thrown off the field, too.

"Weaver is like a nightmare that keeps coming back. To me, he's the Ayatollah of the eighties."

Nick Bremigan, umpire, cherishing argumentative umpire Earl Weaver

⚾   ⚾   ⚾

"How do you know when George Steinbrenner is lying? When you see his lips move."

Jerry Reinsdorf, chairman of the board of the White Sox

⚾   ⚾   ⚾

"Oakland is the luckiest city since Hiroshima."

Stuart Symington, senator from Missouri, bidding farewell to Charlie Finley's Kansas City A's

⚾   ⚾   ⚾

"There was a vacancy when I left, and the owners decided to continue with it."

Happy Chandler, former baseball commissioner, on his successor, Ford Frick

⚾   ⚾   ⚾

"He's so incompetent that he couldn't be crew chief on a sunken submarine."

Billy Martin on umpire Jerry Neu-decker

Ⓜ   Ⓜ   Ⓜ

"When Charlie Finley had his heart operation, it took eight hours—seven just to find his heart."

Steve McCatty, A's right-hander, had no love for his boss

Ⓜ   Ⓜ   Ⓜ

"I want the Reds. I want to take Pete Rose's ugly face and stick it in the mud."

Billy Martin, in January of 1977, states his preference for a World Series opponent that year. The Yankees had lost the previous World Series to the Reds, four games to none. In 1977 they would get the Dodgers, four games to two.

Ⓜ   Ⓜ   Ⓜ

"It proves no man can be a success in two national pastimes."

Oscar Levant, pianist and wit, on Joe DiMaggio's divorce from Marilyn Monroe

Ⓜ   Ⓜ   Ⓜ

"The evidence suggests he couldn't identify Babe Ruth in a lineup with Alice Cooper, Billy Carter, and Morris, the finicky cat."

Dave Kindred, sportswriter, questions the acumen of Brewers general manager Harry Dalton

Ⓜ   Ⓜ   Ⓜ

"The designated gerbil."

> **Bill Lee, pitcher, makes clear his respect for his Red Sox manager Don Zimmer**

Ⓧ   Ⓧ   Ⓧ

"When Billy Martin reaches for a bar tab, his arm shrinks six inches."

> **Tommy Lasorda prefers not to socialize with his colleague**

Ⓧ   Ⓧ   Ⓧ

"Jim Frey has the emotional intensity of a comatose eggplant."

> **Bill James, sportswriter, doubts the leadership of the Royals' manager**

Ⓧ   Ⓧ   Ⓧ

"Bobby Brown reminds me of a fellow who's been hitting for twelve years and fielding for one."

> **Casey Stengel on the Yankee player who is now American League president**

Ⓧ   Ⓧ   Ⓧ

"He's the Wizard of Odd."

> **Mike Torrez, like so many others, was less than thrilled to be playing on Charlie Finley's A's**

Ⓧ   Ⓧ   Ⓧ

"Munson's not moody, he's just mean. When you're moody, you're nice sometimes."

> **Sparky Lyle on Yankee catcher Thurman Munson**

Ⓧ   Ⓧ   Ⓧ

"Steve Garvey is not sure whether he wants to be a first baseman or the pope. He's so goody he goes out behind the barn to chew gum."

Don Rickles, comedian and Dodgers fan

"The only thing Reggie can do better than me on the field is talk."

Rod Carew, Angels teammate

"We was going to get him a birthday cake, but we figured he'd drop it."

Casey Stengel on the inept Mets outfielder "Marvelous" Marv Throneberry, 1962

"There are two things George Steinbrenner doesn't know about, baseball and weight control."

Graig Nettles on his former boss

"One's a born liar and the other's a convicted one."

Billy Martin making a double play on Reggie Jackson and George Steinbrenner. Steinbrenner's conviction was for making illegal campaign contributions.

"He has the personality of a tree trunk."

John Stearns, Mets catcher, was real buddy-buddy with teammate Dave Kingman

"He's got a square jaw and a square head, and both match his personality."

Johnny Bench expresses his admiration for Pete Rose

①   ①   ①

"Basically, everyone knows he's a public-relations man."

Ron Cey is less than bowled over by Dodgers teammate Steve Garvey's squeaky-clean image

①   ①   ①

"Dave Parker is so unpopular in Pittsburgh that he could run for mayor unopposed and still lose."

Charley Feeney, sportswriter, sums up public opinion

①   ①   ①

"There isn't enough mustard in the world to cover Reggie Jackson."

Darrold Knowles, A's pitcher, finds a new way to accuse Jackson of being a hotdogger

①   ①   ①

"Mike Anderson's limitations are limitless."

Danny Ozark, while managing the Phillies, had a problem with his outfield

①   ①   ①

"It's not that Reggie is a bad outfielder. He just has trouble judging the ball and picking it up."

Billy Martin, Yankee coach, on Reggie Jackson's skills in right field

①   ①   ①

"He looks like he got here on a raft."

Vin Scully, broadcaster, describing skinny reliever Pat Zachary as he came into a game

⊗   ⊗   ⊗

"You've gone from a human vacuum cleaner to a litter-bug."

Dave McNally, pitcher for the Orioles, chides Brooks Robinson after the great third baseman made a series of errors at the start of the 1974 season

⊗   ⊗   ⊗

"Wagner is the only man I've ever seen who could tie his shoelaces without bending over."

Lefty Gomez on bowlegged Honus Wagner

⊗   ⊗   ⊗

"Leo Durocher is a man with an infinite capacity for making a bad thing worse."

Branch Rickey is down on his manager

⊗   ⊗   ⊗

"Tommy's the only manager in the major leagues who uses a fork for a letter opener."

Rick Monday on his manager Tommy Lasorda's paunch

⊗   ⊗   ⊗

"Let's put it this way—pigeons have been roosting on him for two years."

Vin Scully, sportscaster, on Ron Cey's vanished agility at third base

⊗   ⊗   ⊗

"I'm much more sexual than my husband. I need a man more than he needs a woman."

Cyndy Garvey, interviewed in *Inside Sports* in 1980 about her troubled marriage to Steve Garvey

Ⓧ   Ⓧ   Ⓧ

"That's pretty good, considering Dave's previous idol was himself."

Willie Stargell, upon being informed that Dave Parker had said Stargell was his idol

Ⓧ   Ⓧ   Ⓧ

"When you unwrap one, it tells you how good it is."

Catfish Hunter describes the Reggie Bar

Ⓧ   Ⓧ   Ⓧ

"Pour hot water over a sportswriter and you'll get instant bleep."

Ted Williams

Ⓧ   Ⓧ   Ⓧ

"It's a boring job. But people who become coaches are not easily bored. You ever see a baby play with a rattle for two hours?"

Jim Bouton gives it to the coaches in *Ball Four*

Ⓧ   Ⓧ   Ⓧ

"He really believes that he made a winning team out of Pete Rose, Johnny Bench, Joe Morgan, George Foster, and Davey Concepcion by teaching them the virtues of shiny shoes and clean upper lips."

Bill James, sportswriter, takes Sparky Anderson's emphasis on good grooming with a grain of salt

Ⓧ   Ⓧ   Ⓧ

"You can plant two thousand rows of corn with the fertilizer Lasorda spreads around."

Joe Garagiola, sportscaster, is equally dubious about Tommy Lasorda's "Great Dodger in the Sky" routines

⚾   ⚾   ⚾

"The Cubs striking is about as significant as the buggy-whip manufacturers going on strike. What difference does it make?"

Mike Royko, in the *Chicago Sun-Times*, wonders why the Cubs bother during the 1981 baseball strike

⚾   ⚾   ⚾

"He can run, hit, throw, and field. The only thing Willie Davis has never been able to do is think."

Buzzie Bavasi, general manager of the Angels, wants a man who can do everything

⚾   ⚾   ⚾

"Anybody who has plastic hair is bound to have problems."

Jay Johnstone, Dodgers outfielder, has an explanation for why some people dislike teammate Steve Garvey

⚾   ⚾   ⚾

"They move very, very reluctantly. I think it was a long time before any of them had inside plumbing."

Edward Bennett Williams, Orioles owner, blasts the conservatism of National League owners

⚾   ⚾   ⚾

"He was known to play night games no matter what it said on the schedule."

Vic Ziegel, sportswriter, remembers the lifestyle of Joe Pepitone

⚾   ⚾   ⚾

"That Maris. You'd tell him something and he'd stare at you for a week before answering."

Casey Stengel didn't find the home-run king too cooperative

⚾   ⚾   ⚾

"Tell a ballplayer something a thousand times, then tell him again, because that might be the time he'll understand something."

Paul Richards, manager, has a low estimation of players' mental capacity

⚾   ⚾   ⚾

"Most pitchers are too smart to manage."

Jim Palmer, Cy Young Award pitcher, fires another salvo in his running battle with his Orioles manager, Earl Weaver

⚾   ⚾   ⚾

"When they smile, blood drips off their teeth."

Ted Turner, owner of the Braves, thinks agents were nurtured in Transylvania

⚾   ⚾   ⚾

"Everybody knows that Casey Stengel has forgotten more baseball than I'll ever know. That's the trouble. He's forgotten it."

Jimmy Piersall, when playing for the hapless 1963 Mets

⚾   ⚾   ⚾

"He plays the outfield like he's trying to catch grenades."

Reggie Jackson, often criticized for his own outfield play, lets Claudell Washington have it

"Charlie Finley hiring Billy Martin is like Captain Hook hiring the alligator."

Johnny Carson hits two birds with one stone

"Most valuable player from the neck down."

Eddie Stanky, Chicago White Sox manager, begrudges Carl Yastrzemski's 1967 Triple Crown season, and wonders if there is a brain to go with the brawn

8 Ground Rule Doubles

When a fair ball bounces into the stands or is interfered with by a fan, the batter is automatically awarded second base. It's not a home run, but it's not just a single, either. Similarly, many baseball quotes are **Ground Rule Doubles.**

"A fellow bossing a big-league ball club is busier than a one-armed paperhanger with the flying hives."

Ty Cobb, 1914

⚾ ⚾ ⚾

"It isn't really the stars that are expensive. It's the high cost of mediocrity."

Bill Veeck, owner, giving his view of baseball salaries

⚾ ⚾ ⚾

"What scares the hell out of me is waking up dead some morning in the Hyatt Hotel in Oakland."

Earl Weaver explains his decision to retire from managing

⚾ ⚾ ⚾

"My ultimate dream is to have my own bank, maybe in Paris. I'd call it Bank's Bank on the Left Bank."

Ernie Banks, Cubs superstar, on studying finance

⚾ ⚾ ⚾

"The only change is that baseball has turned Paige from a second-class citizen to a second-class immortal."

Satchel Paige sums up the significance of being named to the Hall of Fame's Negro League roster

⊗   ⊗   ⊗

"You gotta have a catcher. If you don't have a catcher, you'll have all passed balls."

Casey Stengel, Mets manager, explains to the press his decision to draft Hobie Landrith first in the expansion draft

⊗   ⊗   ⊗

"I want to make sure nobody is in my uniform."

Don Zimmer, Red Sox manager, had a reason for always arriving early at Fenway Park

⊗   ⊗   ⊗

"I drink a lot of coffee to key up. My wife looks at me in bed. I'm on my back, popeyed, staring up at the ceiling."

Sparky Anderson believes a manager should be nervous before a game

⊗   ⊗   ⊗

"I don't take anything to alter the physiological condition of my body. It's running too perfectly on 82 percent body fat."

Doug Rader, Rangers manager

⊗   ⊗   ⊗

"Some of the younger guys have me eating the tablets and the wrapper."

Davey Johnson discusses his ant-acid habit while manager of the 1984 Mets

⚾   ⚾   ⚾

"Cadillacs are down at the end of the bat."

Ralph Kiner's reply when it was suggested that he could boost his average by choking up on the bat, and hitting for singles instead of home runs

⚾   ⚾   ⚾

"Beer makes some people happy. Cashing checks makes me delirious with joy."

Jim Brosnan, Reds pitcher, in 1961

⚾   ⚾   ⚾

"He'd give you the shirt off his back. Of course, he'd call a press conference to announce it."

Catfish Hunter defending Reggie Jackson, sort of

⚾   ⚾   ⚾

"We've got a problem here. Luis Tiant wants to use the bathroom, and it says no foreign objects in the toilet."

Graig Nettles, nettling the Cuban-born pitcher on a Yankee team flight

⚾   ⚾   ⚾

"I flush the john between innings to keep my wrists strong."

John Lowenstein of the Baltimore Orioles, on keeping fit as a designated hitter

Ⓧ   Ⓧ   Ⓧ

"The trick against Drysdale is to hit him before he hits you."

Orlando Cepeda on Drysdale's brushback pitching

Ⓧ   Ⓧ   Ⓧ

"If you step on people in this life, you're going to come back as a cockroach."

Willie Davis, outfielder, during a dispute with management

Ⓧ   Ⓧ   Ⓧ

"One of my goals in life was to be surrounded by unpretentious, rich young men. Then I bought the Braves and was surrounded by twenty-five of them."

Ted Turner

Ⓧ   Ⓧ   Ⓧ

"With the money I'm making, I should be playing two positions."

Pete Rose

Ⓧ   Ⓧ   Ⓧ

"Tommy's amazing. Why, he'll even talk to numbers on an elevator. When they're lit up, he thinks they're listening."

Don Sutton, pitcher, on garrulous Dodgers manager Tommy Lasorda

Ⓧ   Ⓧ   Ⓧ

"Instead of looking like the American flag, I look like a taco."

Steve Garvey comments on the Padres uniforms, after coming over from the Dodgers

"In Cleveland, pennant fever usually ends up being just a forty-eight-hour virus."

Frank Robinson, former Indians manager

"If I'd known I was gonna pitch a no-hitter today, I would have gotten a haircut."

Bo Belinsky, self-styled glamour boy of the Angels, in 1962

"Noise pollution can't be that much of a problem. There's nothing to cheer about there."

Representative John F. Dunn supports the installation of lights at Wrigley Field, during one of the Cubs' many dismal seasons

"The only way to prove that you're a good sport is to lose."

Ernie Banks looks for the silver lining with regard to the Cubs' record

"We used to go into towns knowing we were good and knowing we would win. Now we think we're good, and we think we're going to win."

Lou Piniella, comparing the 1978 and the 1984 Yankees

"There are so many new faces around here, I thought I'd been traded."

Ken Oberkfell, Cardinals infielder, reacting to the wholesale changes in the team's roster at spring training in 1981

⚾   ⚾   ⚾

"There are only two places in the league. First and no place."

Tom Seaver on the importance of winning

⚾   ⚾   ⚾

"The worst thing is the day you realize you want to win more than your players do."

Gene Mauch, while managing the Twins

⚾   ⚾   ⚾

"Kids should practice autographing baseballs. This is a skill that's often overlooked in Little League."

Tug McGraw gets his priorities in order

⚾   ⚾   ⚾

"I'm proud of them and happy they don't have to work for a living."

Phil Niekro, Sr., cherishing the major-league careers of his sons Joe and Phil Junior

⚾   ⚾   ⚾

"Has anybody ever satisfactorily explained why the bad hop is always the last one?"

Hank Greenwald, sportscaster for the Giants, ponders a mystery of baseball

⚾   ⚾   ⚾

"It is interesting about people that leave early from ballgames. It's almost as if they came out to the ballgame to see if they can beat the traffic home."

Lou Simmons, Oakland sportscaster, has a key to the fickleness of fans

Ⓧ　　Ⓧ　　Ⓧ

"I talk to Tug McGraw in the bullpen all the time. Neither of us has an elevator that goes to the top floor, so mostly we talk from the waist down."

Al Holland, Phillies reliever, on a fellow flake

Ⓧ　　Ⓧ　　Ⓧ

"I don't need that stuff. I've got it all up here."

Billy Martin trusts his brain over computers

Ⓧ　　Ⓧ　　Ⓧ

"Am I worried? How would you feel if you had to hold your breath four times a day for the next two days?"

Jim Frey, Cubs manager, on the hitting ability of Darryl Strawberry, whose talents he had nurtured as a Mets coach the previous year

Ⓧ　　Ⓧ　　Ⓧ

"I'm not sure I'd rather be managing or testing bulletproof vests."

Joe Torre on being manager of the Mets, 1981

Ⓧ　　Ⓧ　　Ⓧ

"It was another laugher."

Davey Johnson, managing the Mets in 1984, after beating the Expos two to one in eleven innings

⚾   ⚾   ⚾

"To a pitcher, a base hit is the perfect example of negative feedback."

Steve Holvey, outfielder

⚾   ⚾   ⚾

"The pitcher has to find out if the hitter is timid. And if the hitter is timid, he has to remind the hitter he's timid."

Don Drysdale, explaining the necessity of the brushback pitch

⚾   ⚾   ⚾

"There are only two innings to go and we're looking good."

Don Larsen, breaking an unwritten rule by taking note of the fact that he had not yet allowed a hit. This was after seven innings of his perfect game in the 1956 World Series.

⚾   ⚾   ⚾

"It's amazing how fast you grow old in this game. At first you're the rookie right-hander; next season you're that promising right-hander; then suddenly you're 'the old man.' "

Don Sutton in 1977

⚾   ⚾   ⚾

"I'm lucky my kids know me. So I'm not going to start a 'get to know Walt Terrell' petition. Besides, as long as the guy making out the checks knows me, I'm fine."

Walt Terrell, Mets pitcher in 1984

Ⓑ　　Ⓑ　　Ⓑ

"Yog, you take a diaper and put it in the shape of a base-ball diamond. Take the baby's bottom and put it on the pitcher's mound. Take first base and pin it to third. Take home and slide it into second."

Jimmy Piersall, former Red Sox outfielder and father of ten children, tells how he instructed Yogi Berra in diapering

Ⓑ　　Ⓑ　　Ⓑ

"I enjoy being a reliever because I like getting six outs for the same money as getting twenty-seven."

Steve McCatty, Oakland A's pitcher

Ⓑ　　Ⓑ　　Ⓑ

"The reason I love baseball so much is because when I come into a game in the bottom of the ninth, bases loaded, no one out, and a one-run lead, it takes people off my mind."

Tug McGraw

Ⓑ　　Ⓑ　　Ⓑ

"I'm not going to agree with them and I'm not going to deny it. I do have a tendency to go to my hat a lot. I guess they figure that's where it is. That's not where it is, though."

Mike Proly, Cubs pitcher, deals with accusations that he doctors the ball

Ⓑ　　Ⓑ　　Ⓑ

"I'd rather hit than have sex."

Reggie Jackson

℗ ℗ ℗

"I'd rather be a swing man on a championship team than a regular on another team."

Lou Piniella, expressing the philosophy that made him one of George Steinbrenner's favorite players

℗ ℗ ℗

"I've found that you don't need to wear a necktie if you can hit."

Ted Williams on the well-dressed baseball player

℗ ℗ ℗

"Fans don't boo nobodies."

Reggie Jackson has his own view of getting booed so often

℗ ℗ ℗

"He's a sinkerball pitcher, and like all things that sink, they tend to get wet once in a while."

Ron Luciano, former umpire, on the doctored pitches of Steve Rogers

℗ ℗ ℗

"A great catch is like watching girls go by. The last one you see is always the prettiest."

Bob Gibson, Hall of Fame pitcher, on the art of the outfielder

℗ ℗ ℗

"I signed Oscar Gamble on the advice of my attorney. I no longer have Gamble and I no longer have my attorney."

Ray Kroc, late owner of the Padres, knew how to correct a mistake

"I throw the ball right down the middle. The high-ball hitters swing over it and the low-ball hitters swing under it."

Saul Rogovin, White Sox pitcher in the 1950s

"The best pitchers have the worst moves to first base, probably because they let so few runners get there."

Tommy Harper, outfielder and dangerous base-stealer, explains a baseball phenomenon

"The first look the Kansas City Royals got at Frederick Joseph Patek, they figured there must be a slow leak at Disneyland."

Jim Murray, sportswriter, has an idea where very short shortstop Patek came from

"Your body is just like a bar of soap. It gradually wears down from repeated use."

Richie Allen, slugger

"You spend a good piece of your life gripping a baseball, and in the end it turns out that it was the other way around all the time."

Jim Bouton, former pitcher, who had a hard time letting go of the game

⚾   ⚾   ⚾

"Was it difficult leaving the *Titanic?*"

Sal Bando, traded by Charlie Fin-ley, figures he landed in a lifeboat

⚾   ⚾   ⚾

"Instead of identifying somebody as their manager, the Yankees should appoint him 'vice-president, dugout de-cisions.' "

Dave Anderson, *New York Times* columnist, on George Steinbren-ner's habit of telling his managers how to manage

⚾   ⚾   ⚾

"I have found that the ones who drink milkshakes don't win many ballgames."

Casey Stengel, defending the hard-liquor man

⚾   ⚾   ⚾

"If I did anything funny on the ballfield, it was strictly ac-cidental. Like the way I played third. Some people thought it was hilarious, but I was on the level all the time."

Rocky Bridges, much-traveled for-mer utility man

⚾   ⚾   ⚾

"I looked in my glove and then on the ground. That left only one other place—the other side of the fence."

> **Pat Kelly, Orioles outfielder, knew a home run when he couldn't find it**

⚾   ⚾   ⚾

"Carrots might be good for my eyes, but they won't straighten out the curveball."

> **Carl Furillo of the Brooklyn Dodgers**

⚾   ⚾   ⚾

"If you don't win, you're going to be fired. If you do win, you've only put off the day you're going to be fired."

> **Leo Durocher, in *Nice Guys Finish Last***

⚾   ⚾   ⚾

"When we lost I couldn't sleep at night. When we win I can't sleep at night. But when you win, you wake up feeling better."

> **Joe Torre, weary from managing the Mets**

⚾   ⚾   ⚾

"It's a lot easier when you're starting, because when you're starting you can pick your days to drink."

> **Bill Lee would rather not be a reliever**

⚾   ⚾   ⚾

"A lot of things run through your head when you're going in to relieve in a trouble spot. One of them was, 'Should I spike myself?' "

> **Lefty Gomez was also dubious about relieving, and often considered the merits of a self-inflicted injury**

⚾   ⚾   ⚾

"I've seen the future and it's much like the present, only longer."

Dan Quisenberry, ace reliever for the Royals, takes the long view

"Amphetamines improved my performance about five percent. Unfortunately, in my particular case that wasn't enough."

Jim Bouton

"If everybody on this team commenced breaking up the furniture every time we did bad, there'd be no place to sit."

Casey Stengel saw no reason for Ron Swoboda to throw things around in the 1963 Mets dugout

"I have a son, and I make him watch the Mets. I want him to know life. It's a history lesson. He'll understand the Depression when they teach it to him in school."

Toots Shor, owner of the restaurant much frequented by New York ballplayers, in 1962

"We prefer 'wham, bam, thank-you-ma'am' affairs. In fact, if we're spotted taking a girl out to dinner we're accused of 'wining and dining,' which is bad form."

Jim Bouton in *Ball Four*

"The trouble with bed checks is you usually disturb your best players."

Dick Siebert, former pitcher, while coaching in the minors

"I look at it this way. Suppose those thirty pitches had been balls? Then I would have had no errors."

**George Brett on his thirty errors
at third base in 1980**

⚾   ⚾   ⚾

"He showed them it was a game, so they locked him up."

**Abbie Hoffman, radical, on Jimmy
Piersall, who spent some time in a
mental institution**

9   *Home Runs*

ome runs are **Home Runs,** on or off the field.

"Baseball is a lot like life. The line drives are caught, the squibbles go for base hits. It's an unfair game."

> **Rod Kanehl, Mets infielder in 1963, when being a Met meant accepting disaster on a daily basis**

Ⓜ   Ⓜ   Ⓜ

"It's what you learn after you know it all that counts."

> **Earl Weaver**

Ⓜ   Ⓜ   Ⓜ

"Sometimes the best deals are the ones you don't make."

> **Bill Veeck, White Sox owner**

Ⓜ   Ⓜ   Ⓜ

"What are we out at the park for, except to win? I'd trip my mother. I'd help her up, brush her off, tell her I'm sorry. But mother don't make it to third base."

> **Leo Durocher has his rules**

Ⓜ   Ⓜ   Ⓜ

"Many fans look upon an umpire as a sort of necessary evil to the luxury of baseball, like the odor that follows an automobile."

> **Christy Mathewson, Hall of Fame pitcher, in 1914**

Ⓜ   Ⓜ   Ⓜ

"Don't find many faults with the umpire. You can't expect him to be as perfect as you are."

Joe McCarthy, Yankees manager, to his players in 1931

⚾　　⚾　　⚾

"So I'm ugly. I never saw anyone hit with his face."

Yogi Berra

⚾　　⚾　　⚾

"The secret of managing is to keep the guys who hate you away from the guys who are undecided."

Casey Stengel

⚾　　⚾　　⚾

"In a way, an umpire is like a woman. He makes quick decisions, never reverses them, and doesn't think you're safe when you're out."

Larry Goetz, umpire

⚾　　⚾　　⚾

"It will revolutionize baseball. It will open a whole new area of alibis for the players."

Gabe Paul, baseball executive, on the Houston Astrodome, the first stadium with artificial turf

⚾　　⚾　　⚾

"I don't know. I never smoked Astro-Turf."

Tug McGraw, pitcher, when asked if he preferred grass or Astro-Turf

⚾　　⚾　　⚾

"All I know is, I pass people on the street these days, and they don't know whether to say hello or goodbye."

Billy Martin, on-again, off-again Yankees manager, 1983

⚾　　⚾　　⚾

"I don't care if the guy is yellow or black or if he has stripes like a fuckin' zebra. I'm the manager of this team and I say he plays."

**Leo Durocher tells his players
Jackie Robinson is playing, period,
in 1947**

Ⓧ   Ⓧ   Ⓧ

"Too many people think an athlete's life can be an open book. You're supposed to be an example. Why do I have to be an example for your kid? *You* be an example for your kid."

**Bob Gibson, Cardinals pitcher, in
1970**

Ⓧ   Ⓧ   Ⓧ

"Man, if I made a million dollars, I would come in at six in the morning, sweep the stands, wash the uniforms, clean out the offices, manage the team, and play the game."

**Duke Snider of the Dodgers takes
a dim view of salary disputes**

Ⓧ   Ⓧ   Ⓧ

"Baseball is very big with my people. It figures. It's the only time we can get to shake a bat at a white man without starting a riot."

Dick Gregory, comedian

Ⓧ   Ⓧ   Ⓧ

"I have only one superstition. I make sure to touch all the bases when I hit a home run."

Babe Ruth

Ⓧ   Ⓧ   Ⓧ

"There are three secrets to managing. The first secret is 'have patience.' The second is 'be patient.' And the third and most important secret is 'patience.' "

**Chuck Tanner, a manager with the
long view**

Ⓧ   Ⓧ   Ⓧ

"The great trouble with baseball today is that most of the players are in the game for the money and that's it—not for the love of it, the excitement of it, the thrill of it."

Ty Cobb, Hall-of-Famer, is ahead of his time in 1925

Ⓜ   Ⓜ   Ⓜ

"Jeez. They're going to give me fifty thousand smackers just for *living*."

Dizzy Dean, after his life story was optioned by Hollywood

Ⓜ   Ⓜ   Ⓜ

"Most people are dead at my age. You could look it up."

Casey Stengel takes pride in being seventy-five

Ⓜ   Ⓜ   Ⓜ

"Don't look back. Something may be gaining on you."

Satchel Paige

Ⓜ   Ⓜ   Ⓜ

"The game's not over till it's over."

Yogi Berra can't be disputed on this one

Ⓜ   Ⓜ   Ⓜ

"I have observed that baseball is not unlike a war, and when you come right down to it, we batters are the heavy artillery."

Ty Cobb

Ⓜ   Ⓜ   Ⓜ

"Good pitching will always stop good hitting and vice versa."

Casey Stengel pinpoints the difficulty of managing

Ⓜ   Ⓜ   Ⓜ

"Ninety feet between bases is the nearest thing to perfection that man has yet achieved."

Red Smith, sportswriter, loved the game

⊗   ⊗   ⊗

"I believe in the Rip Van Winkle theory—that a man from 1910 must be able to wake up after being asleep for seventy years, walk into a ballpark, and understand baseball perfectly."

Bowie Kuhn, Commissioner of Baseball, on his resistance to change

⊗   ⊗   ⊗

"There is always some kid who may be seeing me for the first or last time. I owe him my best."

Joe DiMaggio has a reason for always playing hard

⊗   ⊗   ⊗

"You measure the value of a ballplayer by how many fannies he puts in the seats."

George Steinbrenner puts the businessman's view of baseball as succinctly as anyone

⊗   ⊗   ⊗

"Keep it. I don't want it."

Ray Chapman of the Indians, when told he had another pitch coming from the intimidating Walter Johnson, 1915

⊗   ⊗   ⊗

"We need just two players to be a contender. Just Babe Ruth and Sandy Koufax."

Whitey Herzog, managing the lowly Rangers in 1973, knows just the remedy

Ⓧ   Ⓧ   Ⓧ

"The worst curse in life is unlimited potential."

Ken Brett, Royals pitcher, on his failure to live up to expectations

Ⓧ   Ⓧ   Ⓧ

"Show me a guy who's afraid to look bad, and I'll show you a guy you can beat every time."

Lou Brock, Cardinals outfielder

Ⓧ   Ⓧ   Ⓧ

"When you're hitting the ball, it comes at you looking like a grapefruit. When you're not, it looks like a black-eyed pea."

George Scott, slugging first base-man

Ⓧ   Ⓧ   Ⓧ

"If the guys on the bench were as good as the guys you have out there, they'd be out there in the first place."

Frank Robinson, while managing the San Francisco Giants

Ⓧ   Ⓧ   Ⓧ

"Win any way you can, so long as you can get away with it."

Leo Durocher

Ⓧ   Ⓧ   Ⓧ

"Managing is like holding a dove in your hand. Squeeze too hard and you kill it; not hard enough and it flies away."

Tommy Lasorda, Dodgers manager, waxes poetic

⚾   ⚾   ⚾

"He ain't nothin' till I say so."

Bill Guthrie, umpire, knew who was boss

⚾   ⚾   ⚾

"If the human body recognized agony and frustration, people would never run marathons, have babies, or play baseball."

Carlton Fisk, catcher, who was twice hit in the crotch with a batted ball while crouching behind the plate

⚾   ⚾   ⚾

"Most ballgames are lost, not won."

Casey Stengel

⚾   ⚾   ⚾

"Benedict Arnolds! Betrayers of American Boyhood, not to mention American Girlhood and American Womanhood and American Hoodhood."

Nelson Algren, writer, characterizes the members of the Chicago "Black Sox" who threw the 1919 World Series

⚾   ⚾   ⚾

"There are three types of baseball players: those who make it happen, those who watch it happen, and those who wonder what happens."

Tommy Lasorda

Ⓧ   Ⓧ   Ⓧ

"Whoever would understand the heart and mind of America had better learn baseball."

Jacques Barzun, writer and social commentator

Ⓧ   Ⓧ   Ⓧ

"I'm not sure what it means, but whenever the ball is not in play, somebody grabs his crotch."

Paula Bouton, wife of Jim Bouton, trying to understand

Ⓧ   Ⓧ   Ⓧ

"Baseball is the most unchanging thing in our society—an island of stability in an unstable world, an island of sanity in an insane world."

Bill Veeck, owner

Ⓧ   Ⓧ   Ⓧ

"For the parent of a Little Leaguer, a baseball game is simply a nervous breakdown divided into innings."

Earl Wilson, columnist

Ⓧ   Ⓧ   Ⓧ

"The first big-league game I ever saw was at the Polo Grounds. My father took me. I remember it so well—the green grass and green stands. It was like seeing Oz."

John Curtis, pitcher

Ⓧ   Ⓧ   Ⓧ